Evangelism
1 on 1

**WINNING THE WORLD BACK TO CHRIST
ONE SOUL AT A TIME**

Evangelism 1 on 1 © 2016 by Timothy White, Sr.

All rights reserved. Printed in the United States of America. No part of this book may be used or reproduced in any manner whatsoever without written permission except in the case of brief quotations embodied in critical articles or reviews.

This book is a work of non-fiction. However, names, characters, businesses, organizations, places, events and incidents either are the product of the author's imagination or are used fictitiously. Any resemblance to actual persons, living or dead, events, or locales is entirely coincidental.

For information contact:
info@uptownmediaventures.com

Book and Cover design by Tim White Publishing
Edited by Christine M. Pipic

ISBN: 978-1-68121-104-6

10 9 8 7 6 5 4 3 2 1

Table of Contents

Chapters	Page
Introduction	5
About Evangelism	9
Who?	23
What?	59
When?	69
Why?	83
Where?	93
How?	101
Conclusion	107
About the Author	109

Introduction

There's a misconception going around when it comes to biblical salvation. That we (*the body of Christ*), somehow have the power to save people, the salvation, (*rescuing*) of the physical body is not the same as soul salvation. For example, a person who is drowning can be rescued from certain death which has nothing to do with that individual's soul. Yes, a physical life has been spared, but we are three-part individuals, consisting of body, spirit, and soul. And must learn how salvation works concerning these different aspects.

How people view these three aspects of the body will depend on the culture, and what they choose to accept or reject. The Christian faith is based on the teachings of Jesus Christ, and that's what this book will focus on.

We cannot save anyone; in fact, we need to look very close at what the scripture tells us in the book of Acts when the Holy Spirit was given.

The bible clearly states that **the Lord added to the church** daily such as should be saved (Acts.2: 47), this however does not mean we don't have a part to play in getting people, (*the spiritually lost*), the message of God that can lead them to salvation.

Evangelism 1 on 1

God knows the end from the beginning, so it's important that you and I share our gospel experience with all who will listen.

It's not wise for us to think that salvation comes by our power; it's the Lord who is doing the work in us, and through us.

Salvation is a gift from God to all who will receive it by faith (Ephesians.2: 8-9).

As saints we are called Ambassadors (*earthly representatives*) for Christ (II Corinthians.5: 20), we stand in his place on earth as he is seated on the right hand of the Father in Heaven.

We have been given the ministry of reconciliation, (II Corinthians.5: 18), this is the seed or word of God.

Most people are looking for a reason to reject the Lord; this is done often when the church tries to force Christ on the Individual, love is never forced on people, but rather introduced to them.

This book is about sharing our faith, your faith, by way of practice; it's getting back to the basics and fundamentals of our faith. It's evangelism one on one, it's the simplest way to lead or introduce someone to Christ.

Timothy White Sr.

This book is not about how deep we can appear to be spiritually; it's about surrendering our wills to God, and allowing Him to do, both His will and His good pleasure in us and through us.

In order to help you share more effectively, I have also put scriptures in this book for the purpose of easy access for witnessing. It's so simple that you don't need to have a bible with you, as I included the scriptures referred to in each chapter, at the end of each chapter. For example, you will see the scripture Matthew.28: 19[1] **[find the corresponding passage at the end of that chapter; it will look like this...**

1-Matthew.28: 19].

Once located that scripture reference is written out for ease of access for sharing the word of God, without hunting for a bible, it's that simple.

If you need to quote what the word of God says, this will make it easy for those who do not have a bible close at hand, or might be a little timid or feel inexperienced.

By the way, It's okay if you have another translation of the Bible; the key here is sharing the principles of God's word, not debating over what bible translation is better.

About Evangelism

There's a charge given from the Lord to all believers as He was ending His earthly ministry. That charge was to **"GO"**; this was not a suggestion, but rather a command to His disciples then, as well as now.

This "going", referred to by Christ, was to be productive, result oriented, and would be twofold in nature.

Carefully read over Matthew 28: 19- 20[1] as this will be the basis for this entire book on evangelism. We begin with Salvation, followed immediately by education, (*teaching, instruction*), resulting in our going forth and multiplying, (*bringing forth fruit*), and that the fruit, (*harvest*), should remain.

What kind of fruit are we talking about here? The bible speaks of different kinds or types of fruit. To better understand evangelism, we also need to know a little bit about this fruit bearing.

We first hear about fruit in the Garden of Eden, it was first spoken concerning natural fruit or vegetation, (Genesis.1: 11- 12[2]). It was then used concerning Man, when God created Adam and Eve and placed them in the Garden. Most of the things

Evangelism 1 on 1

we will discuss will be common sense information for application.

God told Adam and Eve to, "be fruitful and multiply"; to bring forth after their kind; the act of **bearing fruit in childbearing** (Genesis.1: 28³).

We are also told from scripture to have the fruit of the Spirit (Galatians.5: 22- 23⁴). God gives to every believer, his Holy Spirit the moment they accept Jesus as their savior (John.1: 12⁵; Ephesians.1: 13⁶).

We are further told, that as believers we are to bring forth fruit; this particular fruit is spiritual, we should have proof as to the result of our spiritual work (*and walk*) in the form of souls converting to Christ, (*this proof is also seen in our lives as they are transformed daily in Christ*).

Jesus tells us that our fruit should remain, (John.15: 16⁷). We are told that without Him, (***Jesus***), we can do nothing (John.15: 5⁸).

Christ told His disciples that they, (*we*), would receive power (*boldness*), after the Holy Spirit has come upon (*to dwell in*) us, and **WE SHALL BE WITNESSES** (*evangelist*) for Him. But Jesus also gave a process that they needed to follow once the Holy Spirit came (Acts.1: 8⁹).

Timothy White Sr.

The first place for them to begin, would also be one of the hardest places to start, Jesus tells His disciples to, **begin their mission at Jerusalem**, (*home*), the place where everyone knows them, (*where people knew them, as well as their past actions and deeds*). They would need boldness to do this, and power that was not earthly, but heavenly and divinely given.

Today, the Lord is still calling men and women who were considered rejects and thought damaged goods. He's calling Men and women from dysfunctional homes with lives of chaos and confusion to serve Him.

Let's take a closer look at one such example. A man who Jesus made an early evangelist for the Kingdom of God.

In the book of St. Mark we are told of a man who was demon possessed, he was in the graveyard, naked crying out and even cutting himself with stones, (Mark.5:1-8[10]), he saw Jesus, (*things change when we encounter Jesus*), he ran and fell down at His feet. As a reminder, there are some people who will **run to** Jesus, as well as those who will **run, from** him.

Jesus healed this man of his spiritual oppression, (*demons*), the man once again sat at Jesus feet, but now clothed, and in his right mind. **Once we**

Evangelism 1 on 1

are cleaned up inside it's also reflected in takes place outside as well.

This man who was once feared, and avoided by the people of the town, had only one desire when he was made whole, he wanted **to follow Jesus**, the one who had cleaned him up (Mark.5: 15[11]), but instead of letting him follow them, Jesus did a remarkable but unusual thing, he gives him an alternative mission.

Jesus tells the man to, **go home**, to go back to the place where the people had once feared and ran away from him.

The mission was clear, Jesus gave him a message (*a testimony*), to give the people when he returned. **GO, SHOW (*proclaim, tell*) WHAT GREAT THINGS GOD HAS DONE FOR YOU** (Mark.5: 18-20[12]). **It was a simple message,** to tell everyone who would listen his experience with Jesus. Yes, the people knew his past condition, but now he could show them his new position and condition, because of Jesus Christ.

This follows the mandate in the scriptures, where we are told, to always be ready to give a reason of the hope that we have in Christ (I Peter.3: 15 [12]).

Timothy White Sr.

Evangelism is most effective, when we keep it simple, when we share what God has done, and is continuing to do, in our lives personally.

How does someone get started evangelizing? It's done by following the simple formula Jesus gives in Acts 1: 8^9, evangelizing begins at home first.

Unfortunately, many believers would rather do it another way, outside and away from their homes first.

The reason for this is often painfully clear. Those at home, know the truth about us, they see what we do, hear what we say, and know where we go when we are not in our holy setting, (*church*). In other words, **they see the true fruit we bare**.

True evangelism can only come by way of true faith, it depends on the surrendering of our wills to God's will, we must remember, that without faith it is impossible to please Him (Hebrews.11: 6^{13}).

We must follow the instructions that we were given by Christ, if we are to be successful in winning, (*leading*), others to the Lord. But there's something more we need to know.

The believers, or saints, must be equipped for the work they are to do, there is a time of preparation, a time to be educated in the things pertaining to God. As believers we are not to **"just go"** based on our

Evangelism 1 on 1

excitement and zeal for God. Zeal can lead us in the wrong direction.

We need to first learn the word of God, if we are to understand the will of God, and then being moved by the Spirit of God. It's then that we become true witnesses for the Son of God. This does not mean we have to know the entire bible, but it's important that we study scripture to learn more about God, Jesus Christ and the Holy Spirit.

Evangelism is done on at least two levels. First, it is for those who don't know the Lord, as it is stated in the great commission, we will elaborate more on that later.

Jesus said He came to seek and to save that (*those*) who are lost (Luke.19: 10[14]), of course this is a spiritual condition the Lord is referring to.

What is lost? It's losing direction, not familiar. One good case of this was that of a young man who wanted his inheritance, (*what he felt he was entitled to*), a young man who wanted complete control of his own life (Luke.15: 11-24[15]).

This was a young man who did not understand what he had, or what he would lose by trying to do things his way, and not trust his father.

This was an important case of why the word of God should be instilled.

Timothy White Sr.

This young man did not come to himself, by himself (vs.17), this could only take place because he was taught all his life how he should live his life, in other words **HE REMEMBERED HIS UPBRINGING**.

The saints of God need to be evangelized as well, in the latter it is to educate the saints in the things pertaining to the Kingdom of God, and instruction in righteousness (II Timothy.3: 16, 17[16]).

This story we call the prodigal, (*lost*) son, is an example of why we must spend time also encouraging one another as we grow in God's word.

Many people are lost emotionally, some physically, but all are lost spiritually, and like the young man in this example, they have no idea how to find that peace, that love, and that Joy that is made available to them by simply getting to know Jesus Christ.

Evangelism reaches people on the emotional, physical, and the spiritual level.

This book deals with issues that seem to frighten so many Christians, when it comes to witnessing for the Lord.

We will keep this as simple as possible, we will examine who, what, when, where, why and how of witnessing (*evangelism*).

Evangelism 1 on 1

Evangelism is not talking about things you don't know, it's sharing what you do know, with others.

1-Matthew 28: 19, 20

[19]Go ye therefore, and teach all nations, baptizing them in the name of the Father, and of the Son, and of the Holy Ghost:

[20]Teaching them to observe all things whatsoever I have commanded you: and, lo, I am with you always, even unto the end of the world. Amen.

2-Genesis.1: 11, 12

[11]And God said, Let the earth bring forth grass, the herb yielding seed, and the fruit tree yielding fruit after his kind, whose seed is in itself, upon the earth: and it was so.

[12]And the earth brought forth grass and herb yielding seed after his kind, and the tree yielding fruit, whose seed was in itself, after his kind: and God saw that it was good.

3-Genesis.1: 28

[28]And God blessed them, and God said unto them, be fruitful, and multiply, and replenish the earth, and subdue it: and have dominion over the fish of the sea, and over the fowl of the air, and over every living thing that moveth upon the earth.

4-Galatians.5: 22, 23

[22]But the fruit of the Spirit is love, joy, peace, longsuffering, gentleness, goodness, faith,

²³Meekness, temperance: against such there is no law.

5-John.1: 12

¹²But as many as received him, to them gave he power to become the sons of God, even to them that believe on his name:

6-Ephesians.1: 13

¹³In whom ye also trusted, after that ye heard the word of truth, the gospel of your salvation: in whom also after that ye believed, ye were sealed with that Holy Spirit of promise,

7-John.15: 16

¹⁶Ye have not chosen me, but I have chosen you, and ordained you, that ye should go and bring forth fruit, and that your fruit should remain: that whatsoever ye shall ask of the Father in my name, he may give it you.

8-John.15: 5

⁵I am the vine, ye are the branches: He that abideth in me, and I in him, the same bringeth forth much fruit: for without me ye can do nothing.

9-Acts.1: 8

⁸But ye shall receive power, after that the Holy Ghost is come upon you: and ye shall be witnesses unto me both in Jerusalem, and in all Judaea, and in Samaria, and unto the uttermost part of the earth.

10-Mark.5: 1-8

Evangelism 1 on 1

¹And they came over unto the other side of the sea, into the country of the Gadarenes.

²And when he was come out of the ship, immediately there met him out of the tombs a man with an unclean spirit,

³Who had his dwelling among the tombs; and no man could bind him, no, not with chains:

⁴Because that he had been often bound with fetters and chains, and the chains had been plucked asunder by him, and the fetters broken in pieces: neither could any man tame him.

⁵And always, night and day, he was in the mountains, and in the tombs, crying, and cutting himself with stones.

⁶But when he saw Jesus afar off, he ran and worshipped him,

⁷And cried with a loud voice, and said, What have I to do with thee, Jesus, thou Son of the most high God? I adjure thee by God, that thou torment me not.

⁸For he said unto him, Come out of the man, thou unclean spirit.

11-Mark.5: 15

¹⁵And they come to Jesus, and see him that was possessed with the devil, and had the legion, sitting, and clothed, and in his right mind: and they were afraid.

12-I Peter.3: 15

¹⁵But sanctify the Lord God in your hearts: and be ready always to give an answer to every man that asketh you a reason of the hope that is in you with meekness and fear:

13-Hebrews.11: 6

⁶But without faith it is impossible to please him: for he that cometh to God must believe that he is, and that he is a rewarder of them that diligently seek him.

14-Luke.19: 10

¹⁰For the Son of man is come to seek and to save that which was lost.

15-Luke.15: 11-24

¹¹And he said, A certain man had two sons:

¹²And the younger of them said to his father, Father, give me the portion of goods that falleth to me. And he divided unto them his living.

¹³And not many days after the younger son gathered all together, and took his journey into a far country, and there wasted his substance with riotous living.

Evangelism 1 on 1

¹⁴And when he had spent all, there arose a mighty famine in that land; and he began to be in want.

¹⁵And he went and joined himself to a citizen of that country; and he sent him into his fields to feed swine.

¹⁶And he would fain have filled his belly with the husks that the swine did eat: and no man gave unto him.

¹⁷And when he came to himself, he said, How many hired servants of my fathers have bread enough and to spare, and I perish with hunger!

¹⁸I will arise and go to my father, and will say unto him, Father; I have sinned against heaven, and before thee,

¹⁹And am no more worthy to be called thy son: make me as one of thy hired servants.

²⁰And he arose, and came to his father. But when he was yet a great way off, his father saw him, and had compassion, and ran, and fell on his neck, and kissed him.

²¹And the son said unto him, Father, I have sinned against heaven, and in thy sight, and am no more worthy to be called thy son.

Timothy White Sr.

²²But the father said to his servants, bring forth the best robe, and put it on him; and put a ring on his hand, and shoes on his feet:

²³And bring hither the fatted calf, and kill it; and let us eat, and be merry:

²⁴For this my son was dead, and is alive again; he was lost, and is found. And they began to be merry.

16-II Timothy.3: 16, 17

¹⁶All scripture is given by inspiration of God, and is profitable for doctrine, for reproof, for correction, for instruction in righteousness:

¹⁷That the man of God may be perfect, thoroughly furnished unto all good works.

Who?

Who should evangelize, and are there special people who do this particular work?

Some would like to believe so, even using scripture to lend support to that belief.

Let's look at the words of Paul to the believers at Ephesus, and He (*The Lord*) gave some, apostles; and some, prophets; and some, evangelist; and some, pastors and teachers; (Ephesians.4: 11[1]).

We need to be very clear as to what Paul is saying here. As we look closer, we can see the "Who" factor Paul is referring to.

It's clear that this book, (*letter*), is to believers, and it is to be used to instruct them further about a few of the functions in the body of Christ.

There is one body (*in Christ*), and one (*Holy*) Spirit and one hope in our calling (*salvation*), One Lord, one faith, one baptism (Ephesians.4: 4- 5[2]).

God has given gifts, (*talents*) to mankind, that these gifts would be used to glorify Him, and edifying the body of Christ by sharing them with others.

Evangelism 1 on 1

Allow me to make a modern-day application, to a scripture spoken by our Lord.

Let your light, (*gift, talent*) so shine before men, that they, *(onlookers, believers, non-believers)* may see your good, (*godly*) work, and glorify the (*your*) Father, in Heaven (Matthew.5:16[3]).

It does not matter what our gift is, it's part of the body, and as we are in the body of Christ all the gifts belong to the Lord.

Every good gift comes down from the Father of lights (James.1: 17[4]) and although the gifts can be used selfishly they still belong to God, who will one day expect an accounting of the gift(s), he has given to us (Romans.11: 29[5]).

Every gift that God has placed in the body, has been placed there to help sustain and maintain the body.

As it is with the natural body, so it is with the spiritual body as well. The natural body must meet certain requirements for its growth, so it is with the spiritual body.

The things our natural body needs are not grown inside us but must be cultivated once they are recognized. There are things that must be obtained before they can be maintained.

Timothy White Sr.

Building materials are a requirement in order to complete any project, and God has given to us the materials we need in order to bring people to the saving knowledge of His Son Jesus.

Evangelism adds to the body of Christ.

Jesus made a very powerful statement in His ministry saying, the harvest (*of souls*) is plenteous, but the laborers (*workers, evangelist*) are few (Luke.10: 2[6]).

Let's not limit evangelism to just the New Testament; it was the root (*heart*) of everything that took place in the Old Testament as well.

To be an evangelist should not be dependent on a definition given by or restricted to what is said in Webster's dictionary. Look for a moment at what happened with Isaiah, he is called a prophet, but he was also an evangelist.

When King Uzziah had died it was then that Isaiah saw the Lord high and lifted up (Isaiah.6: 1-6[7]).

It was a revelation, an experience unlike any before it or after it.

Remarkably, it would be after the king dies that Isaiah would see his true relationship with Almighty God, (*is there anything blocking your vision of God*)?

Evangelism 1 on 1

He, (*Isaiah*) said he was unclean and a man of unclean, (*rebellious*) lips, and dwelled among a people with unclean lips (Isaiah.6: 5).

Isaiah was a big fish if you will, that was caught by the Lord, and he was about to be cleaned up and used by God.

The Lord purged Isaiah's sins; we then hear a question coming from the Lord once Isaiah was cleansed inwardly.

Let's remember also that we need to be cleansed daily from sin. Jesus washed his disciple's feet because they would at times get the stain of sin on them, as they journeyed in this world doing His will (John.13: 9[8]).

Saints are instructed to keep themselves unspotted before the world (James.1: 27[9]). Isaiah was cleansed, but would he accept the call *(his commission)* from God?

Who shall I send (*back to the people who are sinning*), and **who** will go (*speak, prophecy, evangelize*) for us (Isaiah.6: 8[10]).

It's important that we take the limits off the ministry and our service in the Lord.

Timothy White Sr.

As was the response of Isaiah so should ours likewise be; **Here Am I Lord**, send me.

The Christian life is not one that involves seeking to be like Peter, James, John, or even Paul. **Who** then are we to be like?

Christ is the example we are to follow. What were Jesus' first words to those who would become His disciples, He said, **follow** (*be trained, taught by*) me, and I will make you fishers (*catchers*) of men (Matthew.4: 19[11]).

Special note: *Just because we have been doing something for a long time does not mean that we know what we are doing.*

Timing, place and knowledge make the greatest difference when it comes to effectiveness in doing Gods will.

Obedience brings blessings

In order to be most effective in the Lord's work it's vital that we give not only our lives to Him, but our thoughts as well, we are being told, bringing every thought into subjection (*surrendered*) to Him (II Corinthians.10: 5[12]).

As Jesus is our ultimate example in all things, what can we learn from Him about evangelism? We are looking at the **"who"** of evangelism, so we need

Evangelism 1 on 1

to begin with who sent Jesus and who is it that is sending saints today?

Jesus lets us know that the Father had sent Him (John.12: 49[13]; 17: 21, 25[14]), and Jesus is likewise sending us, (John.20: 21[15]).

Christ was in the beginning with the Father, (John.1:1-14[16]) and he and the Father were always in agreement with one another (I John.5: 7-9[17]). The word of God has to first go out before, it can come back in with results.

When sin entered into the world because of man's rebellion (*disobedience*), it became necessary for God to intervene, if man would ever be reconciled back to Him.

God was in Christ, reconciling the world back to Himself (II Corinthians.5: 19[18]).

Who was the guiding force (*power*) behind everything Christ did or would do, it was God the Father (John.8: 28[19])?

You and I are merely to restate the events as they have been given to us from the word of God, and by the Spirit of God, by way of the personal experiences we have with God. Most people would call these experiences **our testimony**.

Timothy White Sr.

Remember the man in the tombs, he was given a testimony once he experienced Christ's love, and he was given a mission.

Everyone God picks up, and cleans up, He will also prepare them and send them out, more of this amazing process later in the book.

If we are to learn from Jesus' example, then let's look at when he began His adult ministry. In Luke's record of the gospel we find some very interesting things taking place in just the first 4 chapters (*which covers 30 years of Christ life from birth to His ministry beginning*).

I would like for you to look at the events that took place once Jesus went to the Jordan River, and was baptized by John the Baptist. I believe this can help us to see a very clear picture of the work, and ministry of Christ.

The birth of Christ was by the work of the Holy Spirit (Matthew.1: 18[20]), we are told that Jesus grew in the Spirit having favor with God and man (Luke.2: 39-41[21]), the Spirit descended on Him like a dove (Luke.3: 22[22]), and we find after he was baptized he was driven by the Spirit into the wilderness where He would be tempted by the Devil (Mark.1: 12[23]; Luke.4:1[24]).

Some of you might ask, what does this have to do with Evangelism? Please consider the following,

Evangelism 1 on 1

Satan had one plan, and it was to get Jesus to sin, to have him sidetracked from the mission He was sent to do.

Satan had been watching Jesus just as he had been watching Job, and as he watches you and I, and what he saw was a sinless life in Christ. Jesus was a threat to everything Satan had established. The whole world was in wickedness (I John.5: 18-20[25]) and Satan wanted to keep it that way.

Here's where you and I need to be very careful. Satan would like for us to believe we are not qualified to share God's word, that we have to be a certain kind of person, and from a special background, that we don't have the gift of evangelism, and that we are not in that part of the body of Christ.

It's my prayer that by the end of this book, you will see things differently as it pertains to evangelism.

Jesus said that he came to seek and save those who were lost, once they are found, they must be re-educated, they must be taught to be better, and do better. But also to reach out to others who were like themselves. This is evangelizing.

There was a man of God called Stephen, the word of God teaches us that he was one of the early saints of God, chosen as a deacon in the first church, one of the qualities he had to have was that he was a man full of the Holy Spirit (Acts.6: 5[26]), are you beginning to see a picture unfolding here, **evangelism is spiritual.**

We find that Stephen was not a person who just looked at the ministry of Christ as being consigned to one place, he was more than a deacon, he was a child of God, and Stephen did not limit God.

Evangelism is stepping out of self.

Stephen with boldness of the Holy Spirit stood up and shared his faith with those who rejected Christ.

Stephen's greatest battle came by way of the religious people, and unfortunately it would bring about his death, (Acts.7: 56-58[27]) but later we find his death would be key in bringing the Apostle Paul to the Lord, (Acts.21: 19-21[28]).

Religious does not mean righteous.

There are many religious people in the world that feel they are doing God's will, but the scriptures show differently.

Evangelism 1 on 1

There was also another man named Phillip who likewise was a deacon in the first church, we find Phillip going to Samaria (Acts.8:4-14[29]) where he challenged the Samaritans with the word of God to accept Jesus as their Lord.

Evangelism is not selfish but selfless.

We find Phillip again as he is led by the Spirit of God down towards Gaza.

Evangelism is effective only when it is done in and by the Spirit of God.

Evangelism is very specific, and it is not random.

Look at what the Spirit told Phillip to do, the command was very specific and deliberate (Acts.8: 26-35[30]).

A Eunuch was returning from worship, and was sitting reading aloud the word of God, but did not understand the message as he was reading.

Philip was instructed to **go and join him**, note that Phillip was not about to miss this opportunity, he ran to him asking as he approached if the eunuch understood what was being said. Here is where true evangelism takes place.

It was clear that the Spirit of God was moving and shining in Phillips life, he was asked to sit and share with him.

Evangelism is sharing what we know with others about Christ.

Phillip didn't have to go searching for something spectacular to say, he was provided with the tools he needed when he arrived, look closely at what Phillip did.

Phillip did not gloss over what the eunuch was reading or take him to another place that Phillip might feel comfortable with sharing, but instead Phillip began at the same place in scripture and preached to him Jesus, (Acts.8: 35[30*]). This is one of the many reasons why it's important to know God's word.

Phillip did not wait to get the eunuch back to Jerusalem so the elders could lay hands on him; **Phillip did not wait** for a special time to baptize him, or say it was not his job to do so, the priority is, was, and always will be the salvation of souls.

Who is to be an evangelist? All of us are to be one on a rudimentary level, it does not matter that we are male or female, young or old, black or white, rich or poor.

Evangelism 1 on 1

Some of the first evangelists were women, far too long we have played down the effectiveness of women by the Lord in ministry, women were first given the message of the resurrection to take back to the disciples (Luke.24: 1-10[31]; John.20: 15-17[32]).

The woman at the well was to be the evangelist to her people, speaking of the greatness of God, when she left her water pot and went to the city saying, come see a man who told me everything I had done, (John.4: 1-30[33]). An evangelist is someone who shares the good news of God's word, salvation, grace, repentance and even mercy.

The apostle Paul told his son in the faith Timothy, to do the work of an evangelist, (II Timothy.4: 5[34]).

Wait a minute, wasn't Timothy a pastor, yet Paul is instructing him to do the work of an evangelist, and to make full work (*proof*) of his ministry, (*manner of living*).

Being a pastor does not exempt a person from evangelism. Evangelism is not about how many people we can invite to our church to hear our preacher, but rather inviting them to receive Jesus as their personal Savior.

Now let's go back and fill in a few blanks. We mentioned Paul's words when he tells the believers that God gave "some", early churches depending on the need for these specific gifts.

We live in a time that there should be a greater evangelistic focus, Jesus set the tone when He entered into his ministry, read carefully Luke chapter 4 verses 17 thru 19[35] to see what Jesus did and how we should be about the business of sharing our faith with others modeling ourselves after Jesus.

Whose job is it to evangelize? As we take a quick look at what is known as the great commission, we can see who should do this work, as we review what the Lord says here, I would like for you to compare what Phillip did with the eunuch, and it is a direct connection of what Christ tells his disciples *(a disciple is a student, a follower)* to do.

Evangelism is powerful

The Lord says for the believers to **Go** (Matthew.28: 19), this is the same admonition given to Phillip upon seeing the man reading the scriptures, Jesus said to **teach** (*evangelize*) all nations, that is bring them to the knowledge of Gods saving grace through Jesus Christ. Phillip again fulfills this requirement.

Evangelism 1 on 1

Jesus tells his disciples to teach them (*those who have now come to the knowledge and his saving grace*) to observe all things that He had taught them. Again we can see how Phillip followed the process Jesus had set for his disciples.

The eunuch wanted to know **"who"** Isaiah was referring to in the scripture, and being a man full of the Holy Spirit, Phillip was able to lead the eunuch to the Lord through understanding and accepting God's word.

Phillips instructions even covered the principles of baptism, and the eunuch requested that he be baptized, this parallel's Jesus' commission to his disciples.

Now that we have a better understanding of who should evangelize, in a moment we will learn what evangelism is.

Who should be evangelized?

Everyone, it is not just for those who are without Jesus, it is for those who know Him as well.

Evangelism is a movement; it is a teaching that encourages conversion to a belief and a way of life.

Who should we evangelize?

Everyone of course, the reason is simple, you and I have no clue as to who will accept or reject the will or word of God, you and I have no idea who will be saved, and with that being the case we need to be about our Fathers business.

Who should evangelize?

According to what we have covered so far, each of us have a responsibility to do so.
Evangelism perfects, (*strengthens*) the body of Christ

Try this:

Next time you have a car wash at your church **DON'T CHARGE**, make it free, if they ask why, tell them the Lord cleaned us and we just wanted to do something for the community.

WHO [references]

1-Ephesians.4: 11

[11]And he gave some, apostles; and some, prophets; and some, evangelists; and some, pastors and teachers;

2-Ephesians.4: 4, 5

Evangelism 1 on 1

⁴There is one body, and one Spirit, even as ye are called in one hope of your calling;

⁵One Lord, one faith, one baptism,

3-Matthew.5: 16

¹⁶Let your light so shine before men, that they may see your good works, and glorify your Father which is in heaven.

4-James.1: 17

¹⁷Every good gift and every perfect gift is from above, and cometh down from the Father of lights, with whom is no variableness, neither shadow of turning.

5-Romans.11: 29

²⁹For the gifts and calling of God are without repentance.

6-Luke.10: 2

²Therefore said he unto them, the harvest truly is great, but the labourers are few: pray ye therefore the Lord of the harvest, that he would send forth labourers into his harvest.

7-Isaiah.6: 1-6

¹In the year that king Uzziah died I saw also the LORD sitting upon a throne, high and lifted up, and his train filled the temple.

²Above it stood seraphim; each one had six wings: with twain he covered his face, and with twain he covered his feet, and with twain he did fly.

³And one cried unto another, and said, Holy, holy, holy, is the LORD of hosts: the whole earth is full of his glory.

⁴And the posts of the door moved at the voice of him that cried, and the house was filled with smoke.

⁵Then said I, Woe is me! for I am undone; because I am a man of unclean lips, and I dwell in the midst of a people of unclean lips: for mine eyes have seen the King, the LORD of hosts.

⁶Then flew one of the seraphim unto me, having a live coal in his hand, which he had taken with the tongs from off the altar:

Evangelism 1 on 1

8-John.13: 9

⁹Simon Peter saith unto him, Lord, not my feet only, but also my hands and my head.

9-James.1: 27

²⁷Pure religion and undefiled before God and the Father is this, to visit the fatherless and widows in their affliction, and to keep himself unspotted from the world.

10-Isaiah.6: 8

⁸Also I heard the voice of the Lord, saying, Whom shall I send, and who will go for us? Then said I, Here am I; send me.

11-Matthew.4: 19

¹⁹And he saith unto them, Follow me, and I will make you fishers of men.

12-II Corinthians.10: 5

⁵Casting down imaginations, and every high thing that exalteth itself against the knowledge of God, and bringing into captivity every thought to the obedience of Christ;

Timothy White Sr.

13-John.12: 49

⁴⁹For I have not spoken of myself; but the Father which sent me, he gave me a commandment, what I should say, and what I should speak.

14-John.17: 21-25

²¹That they all may be one; as thou, Father, art in me, and I in thee, that they also may be one in us: that the world may believe that thou hast sent me.

²²And the glory which thou gavest me I have given them; that they may be one, even as we are one:

²³I in them, and thou in me, that they may be made perfect in one; and that the world may know that thou hast sent me, and hast loved them, as thou hast loved me.

²⁴Father, I will that they also, whom thou hast given me, be with me where I am; that they may behold my glory, which thou hast given me: for thou loved me before the foundation of the world.

²⁵O righteous Father, the world hath not known thee: but I have known thee, and these have known that thou hast sent me.

Evangelism 1 on 1

15-John.20: 21

²¹Then said Jesus to them again, Peace be unto you: as my Father hath sent me, even so send I you.

16-John.1: 1-14

¹In the beginning was the Word, and the Word was with God, and the Word was God.

²The same was in the beginning with God.

³All things were made by him; and without him was not anything made that was made.

⁴In him was life; and the life was the light of men.

⁵And the light shineth in darkness; and the darkness comprehended it not.

⁶There was a man sent from God, whose name was John.

⁷The same came for a witness, to bear witness of the Light, that all men through him might believe.

⁸He was not that Light, but was sent to bear witness of that Light.

⁹That was the true Light, which lighteth every man that cometh into the world.

¹⁰He was in the world, and the world was made by him, and the world knew him not.

¹¹He came unto his own, and his own received him not.

¹²But as many as received him, to them gave he the power to become the sons of God, even to them that believe on his name:

¹³Which were born, not of blood, nor of the will of the flesh, nor of the will of man, but of God.

¹⁴And the Word was made flesh, and dwelt among us, (and we beheld his glory, the glory as of the only begotten of the Father,) full of grace and truth.

17-I John.5:7-9

⁷The impotent man answered him, Sir, I have no man, when the water is troubled, to put me into the pool:

Evangelism 1 on 1

but while I am coming, another steppeth down before me.

⁸Jesus saith unto him, Rise, take up thy bed, and walk.

⁹And immediately the man was made whole, and took up his bed, and walked: and on the same day was the Sabbath.

18-II Corinthians.5: 19

¹⁹To wit, that God was in Christ, reconciling the world unto himself, not imputing their trespasses unto them; and hath committed unto us the word of reconciliati

19- John.8: 28

²⁸Then said Jesus unto them, When ye have lifted up the Son of man, then shall ye know that I am he, and that I do nothing of myself; but as my Father hath taught me, I speak these things.

20-Matthew.1: 18

¹⁸Now the birth of Jesus Christ was on this wise: When as his mother Mary was espoused to Joseph, before they came together, she was found with child of the Holy Ghost.

21-Luke.2: 39-41

³⁹And when they had performed all things according to the law of the Lord, they returned into Galilee, to their own city Nazareth.

⁴⁰And the child grew, and waxed strong in spirit, filled with wisdom: and the grace of God was upon him.

⁴¹Now his parents went to Jerusalem every year at the feast of the Passover.

22-Luke.3: 22

²²And the Holy Ghost descended in a bodily shape like a dove upon him, and a voice came from heaven, which said, Thou art my beloved Son; in thee I am well pleased.

23-Mark.1: 12

¹²And immediately the spirit driveth him into the wilderness.

24-Luke.4: 1

¹And Jesus being full of the Holy Ghost returned from Jordan, and was led by the Spirit into the wilderness,

Evangelism 1 on 1

25-I John.5: 18-20

[18]We know that whosoever is born of God sinneth not; but he that is begotten of God keepeth himself, and that wicked one toucheth him not.

[19]And we know that we are of God, and the whole world lieth in wickedness.

[20]And we know that the Son of God is come, and hath given us an understanding, that we may know him that is true, and we are in him that is true, even in his Son Jesus Christ. This is the true God, and eternal life.

26-Acts.6: 5

[5]And the saying pleased the whole multitude: and they chose Stephen, a man full of faith and of the Holy Ghost, and Philip, and Prochorus, and Nicanor, and Timon, and Parmenas, and Nicolas a proselyte of Antioch:

27-Acts.7: 56-58

[56]And said, Behold, I see the heavens opened, and the Son of man standing on the right hand of God.

Timothy White Sr.

⁵⁷Then they cried out with a loud voice, and stopped their ears, and ran upon him with one accord,

⁵⁸And cast him out of the city, and stoned him: and the witnesses laid down their clothes at a young man's feet, whose name was Saul.

28-Acts.21: 19-21

¹⁹And when he had saluted them, he declared particularly what things God had wrought among the Gentiles by his ministry.

²⁰And when they heard it, they glorified the Lord, and said unto him, Thou seest, brother, how many thousands of Jews there are which believe; and they are all zealous of the law:

²¹And they are informed of thee, that thou teachest all the Jews which are among the Gentiles to forsake Moses, saying that they ought not to circumcise their children, neither to walk after the customs.

29-Acts.8: 4-14

⁴Therefore they that were scattered abroad went everywhere preaching the word.

Evangelism 1 on 1

⁵Then Philip went down to the city of Samaria, and preached Christ unto them.

⁶And the people with one accord gave heed unto those things which Philip spake, hearing and seeing the miracles which he did.

⁷For unclean spirits, crying with loud voice, came out of many that were possessed with them: and many taken with palsies, and that were lame, were healed.

⁸And there was great joy in that city.

⁹But there was a certain man, called Simon, which beforetime in the same city used sorcery, and bewitched the people of Samaria, giving out that himself was some great one:

¹⁰To whom they all gave heed, from the least to the greatest, saying, This man is the great power of God.

¹¹And to him they had regard, because that of long time he had bewitched them with sorceries.

¹²But when they believed Philip preaching the things concerning the kingdom of God, and the name of

Timothy White Sr.

Jesus Christ, they were baptized, both men and women.

[13]Then Simon himself believed also: and when he was baptized, he continued with Philip, and wondered, beholding the miracles and signs which were done.

[14]Now when the apostles which were at Jerusalem heard that Samaria had received the word of God, they sent unto them Peter and John:

30-Acts.8: 26-35

[26]And the angel of the Lord spake unto Philip, saying, Arise, and go toward the south unto the way that goeth down from Jerusalem unto Gaza, which is desert.

[27]And he arose and went: and, behold, a man of Ethiopia, an eunuch of great authority under Candace queen of the Ethiopians, who had the charge of all her treasure, and had come to Jerusalem for to worship,

[28]Was returning, and sitting in his chariot read Esaias the prophet.

Evangelism 1 on 1

²⁹Then the Spirit said unto Philip, Go near, and join thyself to this chariot.

³⁰And Philip ran thither to him, and heard him read the prophet Esaias, and said, Understandest thou what thou readest?

³¹And he said, How can I, except some man should guide me? And he desired Philip that he would come up and sit with him.

³²The place of the scripture which he read was this, He was led as a sheep to the slaughter; and like a lamb dumb before his shearer, so opened he not his mouth:

³³In his humiliation his judgment was taken away: and who shall declare his generation? for his life is taken from the earth.

³⁴And the eunuch answered Philip, and said, I pray thee, of whom speaketh the prophet this? of himself, or of some other man?

³⁵Then Philip opened his mouth, and began at the same scripture, and preached unto him Jesus.

Timothy White Sr.

31-Luke.24: 1-10

¹Now upon the first day of the week, very early in the morning, they came unto the sepulcher, bringing the spices which they had prepared, and certain others with them.

²And they found the stone rolled away from the sepulcher.

³And they entered in, and found not the body of the Lord Jesus.

⁴And it came to pass, as they were much perplexed thereabout, behold, two men stood by them in shining garments:

⁵And as they were afraid, and bowed down their faces to the earth, they said unto them, Why seek ye the living among the dead?

⁶He is not here, but is risen: remember how he spake unto you when he was yet in Galilee,

⁷Saying, The Son of man must be delivered into the hands of sinful men, and be crucified, and the third day rise again.

Evangelism 1 on 1

⁸And they remembered his words,

⁹And returned from the sepulcher, and told all these things unto the eleven, and to all the rest.

¹⁰It was Mary Magdalene and Joanna, and Mary the mother of James, and other women that were with them, which told these things unto the apostles.

32-John.20: 15-17

¹⁵Jesus saith unto her, Woman, why weepest thou? whom seekest thou? She, supposing him to be the gardener, saith unto him, Sir, if thou have borne him hence, tell me where thou hast laid him, and I will take him away.

¹⁶Jesus saith unto her, Mary. She turned herself, and saith unto him, Rabboni; which is to say, Master.

¹⁷Jesus saith unto her, Touch me not; for I am not yet ascended to my Father: but go to my brethren, and say unto them, I ascend unto my Father, and your Father; and to my God, and your God.

33-John.4: 1-30

When therefore the Lord knew how the Pharisees had heard that Jesus made and baptized more disciples than John,

²(Though Jesus himself baptized not, but his disciples,)

³He left Judaea, and departed again into Galilee.

⁴And he must needs go through Samaria.

⁵Then cometh he to a city of Samaria, which is called Sychar, near to the parcel of ground that Jacob gave to his son Joseph.

⁶Now Jacob's well was there. Jesus therefore, being wearied with his journey, sat thus on the well: and it was about the sixth hour.

⁷There cometh a woman of Samaria to draw water: Jesus saith unto her, Give me to drink.

⁸(For his disciples were gone away unto the city to buy meat.)

Evangelism 1 on 1

⁹Then saith the woman of Samaria unto him, How is it that thou, being a Jew, askest drink of me, which am a woman of Samaria? for the Jews have no dealings with the Samaritans.

¹⁰Jesus answered and said unto her, If thou knewest the gift of God, and who it is that saith to thee, Give me to drink; thou wouldest have asked of him, and he would have given thee living water.

¹¹The woman saith unto him, Sir, thou hast nothing to draw with, and the well is deep: from whence then hast thou that living water?

¹²Art thou greater than our father Jacob, which gave us the well, and drank thereof himself, and his children, and his cattle?

¹³Jesus answered and said unto her, Whosoever drinketh of this water shall thirst again:

¹⁴But whosoever drinketh of the water that I shall give him shall never thirst; but the water that I shall give him shall be in him a well of water springing up into everlasting life.

¹⁵The woman saith unto him, Sir, give me this water, that I thirst not, neither come hither to draw.

¹⁶Jesus saith unto her, Go, call thy husband, and come hither.

¹⁷The woman answered and said, I have no husband. Jesus said unto her, Thou hast well said, I have no husband:

¹⁸For thou hast had five husbands; and he whom thou now hast is not thy husband: in that saidst thou truly.

¹⁹The woman saith unto him, Sir, I perceive that thou art a prophet.

²⁰Our fathers worshipped in this mountain; and ye say, that in Jerusalem is the place where men ought to worship.

²¹Jesus saith unto her, Woman, believe me, the hour cometh, when ye shall neither in this mountain, nor yet at Jerusalem, worship the Father.

²²Ye worship ye know not what: we know what we worship: for salvation is of the Jews.

Evangelism 1 on 1

²³But the hour cometh, and now is, when the true worshippers shall worship the Father in spirit and in truth: for the Father seeketh such to worship him.

²⁴God is a Spirit: and they that worship him must worship him in spirit and in truth.

²⁵The woman saith unto him, I know that Messiah cometh, which is called Christ: when he is come, he will tell us all things.

²⁶Jesus saith unto her, I that speak unto thee am he.

²⁷And upon this came his disciples, and marveled that he talked with the woman: yet no man said, What seekest thou? or, Why talkest thou with her?

²⁸The woman then left her water pot, and went her way into the city, and saith to the men,

²⁹Come, see a man, which told me all things that ever I did: is not this the Christ?

³⁰Then they went out of the city, and came unto him.

Timothy White Sr.

34-II Timothy.4: 5

⁵But watch thou in all things, endure afflictions, do the work of an evangelist, make full proof of thy ministry.

35-Luke.4: 17-19

¹⁷And there was delivered unto him the book of the prophet Esaias. And when he had opened the book, he found the place where it was written,

¹⁸The Spirit of the Lord is upon me, because he hath anointed me to preach the gospel to the poor; he hath sent me to heal the brokenhearted, to preach deliverance to the captives, and recovering of sight to the blind, to set at liberty them that are bruised,

¹⁹To preach the acceptable year of the Lord.

What?

What is evangelism? Let's start by saying what evangelism is not. It's not about building the local church. Although it will affect the body of believers in their relationship both to Christ, and to one another. So, what's evangelism; it's growing the universal body of Christ. It's putting into practice the principles of faith, as demonstrated and practiced by Christ.

What is evangelism; evangelism is getting out of our comfort zones, our emotional hiding places, and it is putting into practice a willful obedience to the Spirit of God.

What is the purpose of evangelizing?

Evangelism is getting the Word, (*Jesus*), out; it's sharing and demonstrating the ministry of Christ, by way of a transformed life.

Paul speaking to the believers at Rome said, *I beseech (plead, beg) you therefore brothers that you present your bodies a living sacrifice holy acceptable unto God, which is your reasonable (divine, voluntary) service, and be transformed by the renewing of your mind that you may prove* (demonstrate) *what is that good and acceptable, and perfect will of God* (Romans.12: 1, 2[1]).

Evangelism 1 on 1

What does evangelism have to do with me?

Everything, not only does evangelism reach out to others, but it also reaches back in to the one who shares it as well.

Evangelism helps us to grow biblically and spiritually.

Evangelism is turning on the light of Christ in our lives for others to see him by our actions, it's lighting the candle of faith, and putting it on the candlestick for the world that is in darkness to see.

What does evangelism do for others?

It allows the world to see Jesus. We have been told that no man has seen God at any time, but the only begotten Son of God, has declared, (*made*) him known, (John.1: 18^2).

Evangelism puts Christ in the forefront, and the center stage of humanity. Evangelism lifts Christ up, so He can draw all people to himself.

To take it just a bit further, none of us today have seen Jesus, we make Him known by our faith, and that is by way of His Holy Spirit.

Evangelism is also sharing what we think (*hope*) or believe to be true, it is not always fact based. Our spiritual experiences bring about our facts by faith, and this should not be based on our fears or feelings.

I would like to say here that faith becomes fact once it is put into practice, and thereby removing doubts and fear.

Let me give an example here, the two who were traveling on the Emmaus road were heading home and talking about the events that took place concerning Jesus, when Jesus himself joined them (Luke.24: 13-35[3]).

They were questioned about what they were talking about as they traveled, telling Jesus about the things that took place, and that they had hoped that Jesus was the one that would redeem Israel.

Jesus Himself, would evangelize them; Christ wanted to know from them, what they had been talking about that made them so sad, (vs.17). He first wanted them to tell him, what they believed had happened (vs.19).

They told the stranger, what they **had heard** from Jesus' teaching, and how that they had wished that Jesus was the one who would redeem them. "**Them**", meaning Israel, (vs.20, 21), and three days has passed, and they had even heard from some who

Evangelism 1 on 1

went to the tomb, that it was found empty, (vs.22-24). In other words, they were not sure what to believe.

They knew the story (*the words of salvation*), but had not experienced the hope, (*presence or power of salvation*), associated with understanding and applying the scriptures in their lives. They knew the words of the Tanakh, (**Old Testament**), but had no spiritual understanding of it.

Jesus began to explain, (*evangelize*), *to* them how the things they spoke of pertained to Jesus, beginning with Moses and all the other prophets (vs.25-27). A clear understanding was given to them from the word of God, by the Son of God.

Evangelism is simple, and practical, its point is made clear concerning Christ as demonstrated here. Jesus is the Lord's Christ sent to redeem and restore the world back to God.

Evangelism when done properly (*that is in the Spirit*) causes the hearts of those that hear it to burn, (*with excitement and anticipation*), and with great expectation (vs.32).

What is evangelism? It is God excitement; it is the burning inside that leads to a fresher understanding of God's word.

Timothy White Sr.

What is the message of evangelism? It's letting the world know that God has sent His Son to die in our place for our sin, that Jesus took the beating that was meant for us, and by his stripes we are healed.

It's not up to us to try and force people to believe our message. We are to simply share it with others, and allow the Holy Spirit to work in their lives as he has worked in ours.

Try this:

Give out 10 positive compliments to people you do not know during the course of your day today.

WHAT [references]

1-Romans.12: 1, 2

[1]I beseech you therefore, brethren, by the mercies of God, that ye present your bodies a living sacrifice, holy, acceptable unto God, which is your reasonable service.

[2]And be not conformed to this world: but be ye transformed by the renewing of your mind, that ye may prove what is that good, and acceptable, and perfect, will of God.

Evangelism 1 on 1

2-John.1: 18

¹⁸No man hath seen God at any time, the only begotten Son, which is in the bosom of the Father, he hath declared him.

3-Luke.24: 13-35

¹³And, behold, two of them went that same day to a village called Emmaus, which was from Jerusalem about threescore furlongs.

¹⁴And they talked together of all these things which had happened.

¹⁵And it came to pass, that, while they communed together and reasoned, Jesus himself drew near, and went with them.

¹⁶But their eyes were holden that they should not know him.

¹⁷And he said unto them, What manner of communications are these that ye have one to another, as ye walk, and are sad?

[18]And the one of them, whose name was Cleopas, answering said unto him, Art thou only a stranger in Jerusalem, and hast not known the things which are come to pass there in these days?

[19]And he said unto them, What things? And they said unto him, Concerning Jesus of Nazareth, which was a prophet mighty in deed and word before God and all the people:

[20]And how the chief priests and our rulers delivered him to be condemned to death, and have crucified him.

[21]But we trusted that it had been he which should have redeemed Israel: and beside all this, today is the third day since these things were done.

[22]Yea, and certain women also of our company made us astonished, which were early at the sepulcher;

[23]And when they found not his body, they came, saying, that they had also seen a vision of angels, which said that he was alive.

Evangelism 1 on 1

²⁴And certain of them which were with us went to the sepulcher, and found it even so as the women had said: but him they saw not.

²⁵Then he said unto them, O fools, and slow of heart to believe all that the prophets have spoken:

²⁶Ought not Christ to have suffered these things, and to enter into his glory?

²⁷And beginning at Moses and all the prophets, he expounded unto them in all the scriptures the things concerning himself.

²⁸And they drew nigh unto the village, whither they went: and he made as though he would have gone further.

²⁹But they constrained him, saying, Abide with us: for it is toward evening, and the day is far spent. And he went in to tarry with them.

³⁰And it came to pass, as he sat at meat with them, he took bread, and blessed it, and brake, and gave to them.

³¹And their eyes were opened, and they knew him; and he vanished out of their sight.

³²And they said one to another, Did not our heart burn within us, while he talked with us by the way, and while he opened to us the scriptures?

³³And they rose up the same hour, and returned to Jerusalem, and found the eleven gathered together, and them that were with them,

³⁴Saying, The Lord is risen indeed, and hath appeared to Simon.

³⁵And they told what things were done in the way, and how he was known of them in breaking of bread.

When?

When did evangelism begin? It must be noted that the word evangelism appears in scripture only three times, (Acts.21: 8[1]; Ephesians.4: 11[2]; II Timothy.4: 5[3]), but this does not mean it is any less important; in fact, it is the strength, and the heart of the scripture message.

The first message of evangelism is found in the Old Testament; evangelism began the moment man fell from grace in the Garden of Eden. It began with a prophetic statement, *and I put enmity between thee and the woman, and between thy seed and her seed, it shall bruise thy head and thou shall bruise his heel* (Genesis.3:15[4]).

Evangelism is the teaching that separates good from evil, godliness from the unholy, repentance from rebellion; it separates those who walk in the light, from those who choose to walk in darkness.

Moses was an evangelist, he was given a message for Pharaoh, it was simple and clear, tell him to "Let my people go" so they can worship the Lord (Exodus.5:1-5[5]).

God is the creator, and He can use whom He wants. Moses was a man with issues, who not only made excuses for himself, (Exodus.4:1-17[6]), but

Evangelism 1 on 1

Moses also had an unwillingness to go back to do the work of the Lord, because of his past. Remember, Moses killed a man, and this was the reason for his fleeing Egypt in the first place, (Exodus.2: 11-15[7]).

God has a love for mankind so deep, that His desire is that man should not perish (John.3: 16[8]; II Peter.3: 9[9]). So, the Lord had already put in place the means by which the restoration of man could be accomplished. **The God solution,** was prepared from before the foundation of the world, (Ephesians.1: 4[10]), and we see this preparation was observed even back in the Garden of Eden.

When man fell through sin, God implemented His plan to redeem him back to Himself. It would be through His Son, Jesus, the Christ of God.

When does evangelism begin? It begins with us taking the limits off what God can do, and when he can do it. It begins with spiritual acknowledgment of God's word. It's a prepared message given to a prepared people, about a prepared place, the kingdom of heaven, and it is a prepared message for all who call upon the Lord (Romans.10: 13[11]).

Jesus prepared his disciples before He sent them out, He first gave them the example they should follow (John.13: 15[12]).

He also told them He would send them a comforter (*The Holy Spirit*) who would bring all things He said back to their memories (John.14: 26[13]).

Evangelism is not self- oriented, it's Spirit guided.

Time and again we see what happens when the Holy Spirit is moving in the lives of those who trust in the Lord.

Evangelism is allowing the Lord to do His work in us, and then through us, both to do His will and His good pleasure, (Ephesians.1: 9[14] ; Phillipians.2: 13[15]).

When we put our unwavering trust in the Lord, He is faithful to lead us and guide us in the direction of bringing glory to his name through Jesus.

When should **"We"** evangelize? You should do so the moment you are instructed to do so, by the Holy Spirit, this takes place by getting to know God, and having the power of His word in our lives.

When is evangelism most effective? It's most effective when it is done spiritually, and not emotionally?

The Saints are told the natural, (*fleshly, selfish*) man, receives (*does not accept*), the things of God,

Evangelism 1 on 1

neither can he know, (*appreciate*) them, they are spiritually discerned, (*understood spiritually only*). I Corinthians.2: 14[16].

When to evangelize is important, it's about timing, and a surrendered will, as we witnessed with Phillip earlier, and its being guided by the Holy Spirit.

Evangelism is not just going and throwing the seeds of God's word just anywhere, we are instructed not to cast our pearls, (the word of God) among swine, (*those who have no desire to hear or know God's word*). (Matthew.7: 6[17])

We are not instructed to debate, or argue our faith, but to simply sow, (plant) the word of God. One plants, another waters, but it's God who gives the increase (I Corinthians.3: 7, 8[18]).

When are we to share? We are to share when the Spirit says to do so, people might be ready to hear, but might not be willing to change at that moment. But what's important is that we are obedient to God in our willingness to share the gospel with the lost, when told to do so, and at the time we are instructed by the Holy Spirit to move.

The word of God tells us there is a time for everything that takes place, there is a season and a time and purpose for everything under the sun (Ecclesiastes. 3: 1^{19})

Try this:

Memorize one scripture a week for one month (*only 4*) you will be surprised how it will change your life.

WHEN [reference]

1-Acts.21: 8

⁸And the next day we that were of Paul's company departed, and came unto Caesarea: and we entered into the house of Philip the evangelist, which was one of the seven; and abode with him.

2-Ephesians.4: 11

¹¹And he gave some, apostles; and some, prophets; and some, evangelists; and some, pastors and teachers;

3-II Timothy.4: 5

⁵But watch thou in all things, endure afflictions, do the work of an evangelist, make full proof of thy ministry.

Evangelism 1 on 1

4-Genesis.3: 15

¹⁵And I will put enmity between thee and the woman, and between thy seed and her seed; it shall bruise thy head, and thou shalt bruise his heel.

5-Exodus.5: 1-5

¹And afterward Moses and Aaron went in, and told Pharaoh, Thus saith the LORD God of Israel, Let my people go, that they may hold a feast unto me in the wilderness.

²And Pharaoh said, Who is the LORD, that I should obey his voice to let Israel go? I know not the LORD, neither will I let Israel go.

³And they said, The God of the Hebrews hath met with us: let us go, we pray thee, three days' journey into the desert, and sacrifice unto the LORD our God; lest he fall upon us with pestilence, or with the sword.

⁴And the king of Egypt said unto them, Wherefore do ye, Moses and Aaron, let the people from their works? get you unto your burdens.

⁵And Pharaoh said, Behold, the people of the land now are many, and ye make them rest from their burdens.

6-Exodus.4: 1-17

¹And Moses answered and said, But, behold, they will not believe me, nor hearken unto my voice: for they will say, The LORD hath not appeared unto thee.

²And the LORD said unto him, What is that in thine hand? And he said, A rod.

³And he said, Cast it on the ground. And he cast it on the ground, and it became a serpent; and Moses fled from before it.

⁴And the LORD said unto Moses, Put forth thine hand, and take it by the tail. And he put forth his hand, and caught it, and it became a rod in his hand:

⁵That they may believe that the LORD God of their fathers, the God of Abraham, the God of Isaac, and the God of Jacob, hath appeared unto thee.

Evangelism 1 on 1

⁶And the LORD said furthermore unto him, Put now thine hand into thy bosom. And he put his hand into his bosom: and when he took it out, behold, his hand was leprous as snow.

⁷And he said, Put thine hand into thy bosom again. And he put his hand into his bosom again; and plucked it out of his bosom, and, behold, it was turned again as his other flesh.

⁸And it shall come to pass, if they will not believe thee, neither hearken to the voice of the first sign, that they will believe the voice of the latter sign.

⁹And it shall come to pass, if they will not believe also these two signs, neither hearken unto thy voice, that thou shalt take of the water of the river, and pour it upon the dry land: and the water which thou takest out of the river shall become blood upon the dry land.

¹⁰And Moses said unto the LORD, O my LORD, I am not eloquent, neither heretofore, nor since thou hast spoken unto thy servant: but I am slow of speech, and of a slow tongue.

Timothy White Sr.

¹¹And the LORD said unto him, Who hath made man's mouth? or who maketh the dumb, or deaf, or the seeing, or the blind? have not I the LORD?

¹²Now therefore go, and I will be with thy mouth, and teach thee what thou shalt say.

¹³And he said, O my LORD, send, I pray thee, by the hand of him whom thou wilt send.

¹⁴And the anger of the LORD was kindled against Moses, and he said, Is not Aaron the Levite thy brother? I know that he can speak well. And also, behold, he cometh forth to meet thee: and when he seeth thee, he will be glad in his heart.

¹⁵And thou shalt speak unto him, and put words in his mouth: and I will be with thy mouth, and with his mouth, and will teach you what ye shall do.

¹⁶And he shall be thy spokesman unto the people: and he shall be, even he shall be to thee instead of a mouth, and thou shalt be to him instead of God.

¹⁷And thou shalt take this rod in thine hand, wherewith thou shalt do signs.

Evangelism 1 on 1

7-Exodus.2: 11-15

^{11}And it came to pass in those days, when Moses was grown, that he went out unto his brethren, and looked on their burdens: and he spied an Egyptian smiting a Hebrew, one of his brethren.

^{12}And he looked this way and that way, and when he saw that there was no man, he slew the Egyptian, and hid him in the sand.

^{13}And when he went out the second day, behold, two men of the Hebrews strove together: and he said to him that did the wrong, Wherefore smitest thou thy fellow?

^{14}And he said, Who made thee a prince and a judge over us? intendest thou to kill me, as thou killedst the Egyptian? And Moses feared, and said, Surely this thing is known.

^{15}Now when Pharaoh heard this thing, he sought to slay Moses. But Moses fled from the face of Pharaoh, and dwelt in the land of Midian: and he sat down by a well.

8-John.3: 16

¹⁶For God so loved the world, that he gave his only begotten Son, that whosoever believeth in him should not perish, but have everlasting life.

9-II Peter.3: 9

⁹The Lord is not slack concerning his promise, as some men count slackness; but is longsuffering to us-ward, not willing that any should perish, but that all should come to repentance.

10-Ephesians.1: 4

⁴According as he hath chosen us in him before the foundation of the world, that we should be holy and without blame before him in love:

11-Romans.10: 13

¹³For whosoever shall call upon the name of the Lord shall be saved.

12-John.13: 15

¹⁵For I have given you an example, that ye should do as I have done to you.

Evangelism 1 on 1

13-John.14:26

²⁶But the Comforter, which is the Holy Ghost, whom the Father will send in my name, he shall teach you all things, and bring all things to your remembrance, whatsoever I have said unto you.

14-Ephesians.1: 9

⁹Having made known unto us the mystery of his will, according to his good pleasure which he hath purposed in himself:

15-Phillipians.2: 13

¹³For it is God which worketh in you both to will and to do of his good pleasure.

16- I Corinthians.2: 14

¹⁴But the natural man receiveth not the things of the Spirit of God: for they are foolishness unto him: neither can he know them, because they are spiritually discerned.

17-Matthew.7: 6

6 Give not that which is holy unto the dogs, neither cast ye your pearls before swine, lest they trample them under their feet, and turn again and rend you.

Timothy White Sr.

18-I Corinthians.3: 7, 8

7 So then neither is he that planteth any thing, neither he that watereth; but God that giveth the increase.

8 Now he that planteth and he that watereth are one: and every man shall receive his own reward according to his own labour.

19-Ecclessasties.3: 1, 2

3 To every thing there is a season, and a time to every purpose under the heaven:

2 A time to be born, and a time to die; a time to plant, and a time to pluck up that which is planted;

Why?

Why should we evangelize? We should evangelize because **it's part of our love duty**. God so loved the world that he gave His only begotten Son, that whoever believes in Him should not perish, but have everlasting life (John.3: 16[1])

We love Him, God, because He first loved us (I John.4: 19[2]). Evangelism is one way that the Lord lets the world know through His saints, that they can be forgiven for all their sins, receive everlasting life, and reside in Heaven with him and his Son Jesus.

Evangelism is God's love reaching out to the world, through His Saints
Why do we evangelize? The answer is very simple. The lost don't come to us, we must go to them. The bible teaches that we all like sheep have gone astray (Psalms.119: 176[3]; Isaiah 53: 6[4]).

God's desire is that all be brought back to or into the fold (Matthew.18: 12[5]), the reason why is clear, **BECAUSE GOD LOVES US ALL**. Why then are we so afraid to evangelize?

As human beings we are afraid of rejection, it's a basic fear that people will hurt our feelings, or that we will say the wrong thing. Fear was the problem Moses had also, if our humanity gets in the way of

Evangelism 1 on 1

our service to the Lord, it can stall but not stop our ministry as we move forward.

Everyone wants to be successful in whatever they do, it's part of human nature, we don't like to make mistakes, but if God is to use us, we must learn to lean and depend on him (Proverbs.3: 5-6[6]), and to allow the Holy Spirit to guide our walk, words, and witness, and even help us through the mistakes we will surely make along the way.

Why don't we see results for the work we have done sometimes? It's important that we understand that we are here to please the Lord, and not ourselves, but if we are living in the Spirit, we will experience the Love of God as well as the joy that is associated with doing God's will, and not concern ourselves with how well we might be doing.

Fear is often associated with failure or the fear of failing; it's one of Satan's better tricks to get us to believe we are not qualified for the task before us. In part that is true, we are not qualified in ourselves to do anything but sin, all our righteousness the bible says, is as filthy rags (Isaiah.64: 6[7]).

Jesus said without him we can do nothing. He was referring to our need to depend on the Holy Spirit, who The Father would send, and who would bring all things Jesus said back to our memory, (John.16: 13-15[8]).

Timothy White Sr.

We will not, and cannot evangelize on our own. In other words, as we walk in the flesh, and live in the flesh, we will not witness for the Lord, it's against our fleshly desire to do so. We cannot walk forward and backwards at the same time.

We evangelize because we are the eyes, ears, hands and feet for the Lord, and it's because of this, that you and I are here and doing the things we do in Christ.

Why do we evangelize; we evangelize because of the lost, the confused, and the downtrodden, we do so because it's through, and by this method, the Lord is calling the lost to himself.

What should we say, what should we tell them? The message is this, tell them that Jesus died for them, according to the scriptures, and that he was buried, and that after three days He rose again according to the scriptures (I Corinthians.15: 3, 4[9]).

We should tell the lost that God's love is so great for them that He sent his only begotten Son to give His life, just for them (John.3: 36[10]).

The message should be that even though we are sinners and were on our way to a burning Hell, God atoned for our sins through His Son Jesus, and if they receive Jesus as their personal Savior they will never perish (John.3: 15[11]).

Evangelism 1 on 1

We evangelize the saints as well so they would grow stronger in the grace of the Lord Jesus Christ (II Peter.3: 18[12]).

We evangelize the believers that they may be encouraged, and that they would become and remain steadfast and unshakable in their faith.

It's been said that we spend time encouraging one another because it's like going to the gas station to get a fill up, so that we can continue on our spiritual journey (*mission*) in Christ.

By the way, did you know that everything that takes place in our lives is so that we can share with others the glory of God we experience, and so that even our suffering would become a blessing to others of how God can deliver them as well (II Corinthians.1: 3-4[13])?

One of the most important keys to evangelism is the one who's doing the evangelizing.

We don't have to have all the books of the bible memorized. But we do need to spend time in prayer and studying God's word. And as we do this, it becomes easier to discern when the Holy Spirit is moving in our lives, and why.

Timothy White Sr.

Why do we evangelize? It becomes clearer as we experience souls repenting, and accepting Christ as their Lord and savior?

Sincere questions will lead to honest answers, and as we continue down the path of learning the word of God, the Spirit of God opens not only our hearts, but our understanding of what it means to be divinely Loved by God.

Why do we evangelize? Because God loved us, and sent his Son to die for us? Ask yourself this question, why would a parent continue to do for a child who is resentful, rebellious and even hateful. The answer is simple, its done out of love, even when the parents have to discipline them. Evangelism is done out of love.

Try this:

Listen carefully to those around you, don't listen to respond or give an answer, just listen and allow the Lord to show you how to minister to them, and how listening ministers to you as well.

Evangelism 1 on 1

WHY [references]

1-John.3: 16

[16]For God so loved the world, that he gave his only begotten Son, that whosoever believeth in him should not perish, but have everlasting life.

2-I John.4: 19

[19]We love him, because he first loved us.

3-Psalms.119: 176

[176]I have gone astray like a lost sheep; seek thy servant; for I do not forget thy commandments.

4-Isaiah.53: 6

[6]All we like sheep have gone astray; we have turned every one to his own way; and the LORD hath laid on him the iniquity of us all.

5-Matthew.18: 12

[12]How think ye? if a man has a hundred sheep, and one of them be gone astray, doth he not leave the ninety and nine, and goeth into the mountains, and seeketh that which is gone astray

6-Proverbs.3: 5, 6

⁵Trust in the LORD with all thine heart; and lean not unto thine own understanding.

⁶In all thy ways acknowledge him, and he shall direct thy paths.

7-Isaiah.64: 6

⁶But we are all as an unclean thing, and all our righteousness's are as filthy rags; and we all do fade as a leaf; and our iniquities, like the wind, have taken us away.

8-John.16: 13-15

¹³Howbeit when he, the Spirit of truth, is come, he will guide you into all truth: for he shall not speak of himself; but whatsoever he shall hear, that shall he speak: and he will shew you things to come.

¹⁴He shall glorify me: for he shall receive of mine, and shall shew it unto you.

¹⁵All things that the Father hath are mine: therefore, said I, that he shall take of mine, and shall shew it unto you.

Evangelism 1 on 1

9-I Corinthians.15: 3, 4

³For I delivered unto you first of all that which I also received, how that Christ died for our sins according to the scriptures;

⁴And that he was buried, and that he rose again the third day according to the scriptures:

10-John.3: 36

³⁶He that believeth on the Son hath everlasting life: and he that believeth not the Son shall not see life; but the wrath of God abideth on him.

11-John.3: 15

¹⁵That whosoever believeth in him should not perish, but have eternal life.

12-II Peter.3: 18

¹⁸But grow in grace, and in the knowledge of our Lord and Saviour Jesus Christ. To him be glory both now and forever. Amen.

13-II Corinthians.1: 3, 4

Timothy White Sr.

³Blessed be God, even the Father of our Lord Jesus Christ, the Father of mercies, and the God of all comfort;

⁴Who comforteth us in all our tribulation, that we may be able to comfort them which are in any trouble, by the comfort wherewith we ourselves are comforted of God.

³Blessed be God, even the Father of our Lord Jesus Christ, the Father of mercies, and the God of all comfort;

⁴Who comforteth us in all our tribulation, that we may be able to comfort them which are in any trouble, by the comfort wherewith we ourselves are comforted of God.

Where?

Where are we to begin the task of evangelism and evangelizing? As Jesus was about to ascend to heaven, he was leaving the disciples with some last instructions to follow. Jesus was not sending them back to just hang around, or to just sit around.

They were to wait, but this would only be for another few (10) days, until Pentecost. All Jews prepared for this feast.

The disciples were to wait until they were clothed with power, (*the Holy Spirit*), from on high, (Luke.24: 49[1]). They would receive power, (**note: they did not have to beg, or pray for this power**), it would be given to them as promised, (Acts.1: 8[2]).

Where was it that Jesus told them to wait for this power? At Jerusalem, the home base of their faith. It's very important for you and I to know that our ministries also, begins at home, (*our Jerusalem*), the place that people, friends and family know the truth about us.

Surely the ministry would be easier for them, and us, if we did not have to start at home, it's easier to witness to strangers, and in another location, because they don't know us. But our witness Jesus says, **must** begin at home.

Evangelism 1 on 1

Where do we start? With self, we begin with our walk. Our walk is our first witness, have you examined yourself to this point, did you, like Isaiah hear the Lords call, (*from the word of God*), and have you responded to that call, (*by the Spirit of God*)?

Evangelism is not about just hearing the word of God, but it's about sharing it through **PRACTICE**. It's practical Christian living, as spoken of by James, in the book of James, it's faith by works.

Evangelism is one on one; it's each one reaching one. It's leaving the ninety and nine and going after that one who has strayed. It's living a transformed life, and its having the mind of Christ. (Philippians.2: 5^3).

Where are you in your walk and ministry for the Lord; do those around you know you for your faith, or your fears?

Do those around find encouragement when they spend time with you?

As we become fishers of men, we must learn where the best fish are, in our case, they are at home, (*our families and friends*), but it can be tough to fish at home, (*if we are not willing*), and we can run into some snappers, roughys and a blow fish or two. Fishing at home on the surface can be disappointing.

All these fish can be dangerous if handled improperly. People can be just as dangerous emotionally and physically, if not handled with prayer and fasting.

Fishing at home, might take more time than we are willing to give, but let's remember this also, the earth belongs to the Lord, and all that is in it, (Psalms.24: 1^4). Our fishing is not for relaxation, but rather the soul's salvation. Home, is where we most often find the most difficulties when it comes to the word of God, and Christ.

Where does evangelism begin first? It starts in the heart, (mind). As Saints, our driving force should be to see souls saved, because the Lord has saved us.

Fishing takes time, and a lot of patience, and a little bit of skill as well. and the more we learn about fishing, and what fishing can do, the better we become at doing it, and perhaps catching a few.

Where do we find the best fish, in the case of souls they are everywhere? This is why Jesus said he would make us fishers of men.

This is why we must be in tune with Christ in the power of the Holy Spirit, and we will have a good catch.

Evangelism 1 on 1

Start small, that means learn to listen first, we don't learn by running our mouths but by opening our ears.

When the disciples had toiled all night and were tired and had not caught anything Jesus gave them instructions (*in order to be successful in our ministries we must listen to and follow instructions carefully*).

Jesus asked Peter to go out into the deep waters and let his nets out again; Peter's complaint was they had caught nothing, (*remember obedience brings blessing*), and once Peter did as he was told by the Lord, there was a great catch (Luke.5: 1-7^5).

Consider this, the Lord brought the fish to them, all they had to do was what they were instructed to do, and they received a great catch, LET DOWN THEIR NETS.

Evangelism is focusing on our faith not our fears.

Where does evangelism begin, it all begins at the foot of the cross, where the blood of the Lamb of God was shed for the remission of our sins? Where the ministry will lead us, will depend on where God wants us to go, and what he requires us to do once we are there.

Timothy White Sr.

Evangelism begins with our agreeing with God concerning our sinful condition, and His willingness to forgive us.

It's in the Lord, that we find refreshing living water, where peace flows like a river, and where the impossible for man becomes possible with God.

Evangelism like fishing takes time, don't hurry things

If you are married, start sharing God's love with your spouse, if you have children, share God's love with them as well. Where do you start, by simply letting individuals know how much God loves them, as you are the first example of that love.

Remember this also, God will never put on you more than you can bear, and he will never lead you somewhere he will not be there for you, and with you.

Will we make mistakes? Of course we will, but mistakes are what we learn from? The greatest teacher to be born was Jesus Christ, who showed us that we can accomplish anything even in these fleshly bodies, and how do we know this is true, because Christ did it that we now have no room for excusez.

Evangelism 1 on 1

Try this:

Find a young person in your community that you can take the time to mentor. They are looking for good examples; will you be one for them?

Put your cell phone away for a few hours and spend time actually talking to someone face to face.

Randomly give compliments.

If you use Facebook post only positive things for one week.

WHERE [references)

1-Luke.24: 49

[49]And, behold, I send the promise of my Father upon you: but tarry ye in the city of Jerusalem, until ye be endued with power from on high.

2-Acts.1: 8

[8]But ye shall receive power, after that the Holy Ghost is come upon you: and ye shall be witnesses unto me both in Jerusalem, and in all Judaea, and in Samaria, and unto the uttermost part of the earth.

Timothy White Sr.

3-Phillipians.2: 5

⁵Let this mind be in you, which was also in Christ Jesus:

4-Psalms.24: 1

¹The earth is the LORD's, and the fullness thereof; the world, and they that dwell therein.

5-Luke.5: 1-7

¹And it came to pass, that, as the people pressed upon him to hear the word of God, he stood by the lake of Gennesaret,

²And saw two ships standing by the lake: but the fishermen were gone out of them, and were washing their nets.

³And he entered into one of the ships, which was Simon's, and prayed him that he would thrust out a little from the land. And he sat down, and taught the people out of the ship.

⁴Now when he had left speaking, he said unto Simon, Launch out into the deep, and let down your nets for a draught.

Evangelism 1 on 1

⁵And Simon answering said unto him, Master, we have toiled all the night, and have taken nothing: nevertheless, at thy word I will let down the net.

⁶And when they had this done, they enclosed a great multitude of fishes: and their net brake.

⁷And they beckoned unto their partners, which were in the other ship, that they should come and help them. And they came, and filled both the ships, so that they began to sink.

How?

How do we evangelize? How do we get started? It seems complicated, and I'm not sure how to go about it.

Well, I will see if I can help you a little in that area. One of the biggest problems we face is this, we tend to make things complicated that are not difficult in the first place. And we confuse things as we add our own theories, and beliefs to what the Lord requires of us, (*too much of us in our witness, and too little of Him in our walk*).

For instance, Jesus said if we gave a drink of water to the least of his children then we have done this to Him (Matthew.10: 42[1]). This is simple evangelism, nothing profound here, just obedience.

Think about it, have you seen your neighbor out mowing their lawn, I'm sure you have, or have you on a hot day witnessed the garbage collectors as they picked up refuse from your block?

You could take them a cold bottle of water, or maybe a can of soda (*pop*) to cool themselves as they work, you might add a sticker on it to say Jesus loves them; it's no more than planting seeds. This again, is evangelism.

Evangelism 1 on 1

Do you have to say anything at the time you plant a seed? Not really, it's planting first, the Lord might give you the privilege to cultivate the seed you planted at a later time, if not, He has others who will do so. (*Remember evangelism takes us from our comfort zones*).

Evangelism is inclusive not exclusive.

Evangelism is not always the words we speak, but the actions we take that will or could bring glory to God. Remember, it was giving the drink of water in Jesus name that makes the difference.

Whatever we do we are told do it with joy as unto the Lord (Colossians. 3:23[2])

We should be creative not tricky or deceptive as we evangelize, we're instructed to be wise as serpents but harmless as doves (Matthew.10: 16[3]).

Evangelism is making a friend from someone who was once a stranger.

Try taking someone to lunch (*or dinner*) who cannot afford to pay you back, the world calls these deeds random acts of kindness, God is a very deliberate God, and He has a purpose for everything we do, and that is to bring glory to him, and honor to his Son.

Salvation is not stressful, it's simple, and all that is required of you and I, as saints of God, is to show, and share this grace with others.

It's what people call, "the little things" that have the greatest impact in the lives of others, it's a sign to them that someone is paying attention to them, and cares about them.

Sometimes all it takes is an open ear, a gentle heart, and a kind word to change a life.
Try getting some people together and just pick up the trash in a community that is over run with it, see what impact it will have, people will want to know why you are doing it, and who put you up to it?

It's possibly then, that you have an open door of opportunity, to let them know a little about Jesus, and the hope you have in Him.

Evangelism is not just telling people about Jesus, it's also showing them who He is by what we do, not only by what we say. We are instructed to be doers of the WORD, not hearers only (James.1: 22[4]).

Evangelism is setting the life of Jesus on display in our lives for the world to see. It's letting the light of Christ shine in our lives so brightly, that people see our good works, and WE GLORIFY GOD by our words and actions.

Evangelism 1 on 1

Evangelism is not about force feeding, but rather gently leading, it's encouraging people to turn from sins, and to their Savior, Jesus Christ.

Let's remember the word of God where it says, if I be lifted up from the earth (*world*), I will draw all men unto myself (John.12: 32[5]).

How does evangelism work? It doesn't, if those of us who make our boast in the Lord, do nothing with our faith.

Evangelism is the visible seed of faith, that is planted by Gods people, to produce fruit in its season.

Jesus told us, that every tree would be known by its fruit, (Matthew.7: 20[6]), and we, the branches cannot bring forth fruit except we, abide, (*remain attached*), to the vine, (John.15: 4[7]).

How do we know an apple tree, we find apples on it? **A dead tree does not produce fruit.** We are living, breathing, and walking testimonies of how God loves the world.

How do I evangelize? By turning on the light of Christ, so that others can see it, and by becoming a doer of the word of God, not just a hearer.

Try this:

Timothy White Sr.

Next time you go to a fast food restaurant (*inside*) pay the next persons tab (*in back of you*).

Try cutting your neighbors grass when you cut yours.

Strike up a friendly conversation with a neighbor you don't know, it cost nothing, but could have an eternal result.

HOW [references]

1-Matthew.10: 42

[42] And whosoever shall give to drink unto one of these little ones a cup of cold water only in the name of a disciple, verily I say unto you, he shall in no wise lose his reward.

2-Colossians 3:23

And whatsoever ye do, do it heartily, as to the Lord, and not unto men;

Evangelism 1 on 1

3-Matthew.10: 16

^{16}Behold, I send you forth as sheep in the midst of wolves: be ye therefore wise as serpents, and harmless as doves.

4-James.1: 22

^{22}But be ye doers of the word, and not hearers only, deceiving your own selves.

5-John.12: 32

^{32}And I, if I be lifted up from the earth, will draw all men unto me.

6-Matthew 7:20

Wherefore by their fruits ye shall know them.

7-John 15:4

Abide in me, and I in you. As the branch cannot bear fruit of itself, except it abide in the vine; no more can ye, except ye abide in me.

Conclusion

The power of evangelism is not in knowing what to say, but how, and when to say it. It means being tuned in to God, by His Holy Spirit.

This book was not written as the end all for evangelism, it's only a tool that I hope has helped each of you to get more in touch with the Spirit of God, and allow Him to show you how to reach people for the Lord, on a simplistic level.

It is not important that you know, or use every scripture; you can be a great witness for the Lord, if you know how to practice one scripture, and share it properly.

Be mindful of this also; a tool, is used by its handler to help bring about and complete a project. Let's not depend on the tools, but the ability to use them to get the best, and desired results, at the proper time.

What am I saying here, simply this, don't put your dependence on this book, but trust in the Lord, that He, will show you how to use the material in this book as a tool, as you surrender yourself to Him. And that you will learn how to hear His voice, and fulfill

Evangelism 1 on 1

His will in your life as you share His word with others.

Make full proof of your ministry we are told, and each of us has been given an assignment from the Lord Jesus Christ, and this is simply Evangelism 101. It's up to you to take it to the next level, whatever level that the Lord has for you, and your spiritual ministry.

Evangelism is not difficult, it only requires those who know the word of God to share it, it's how we will win the world back to Christ one soul at a time.

About the Author

Timothy White Sr. has impacted thousands of people throughout the world as an author, teacher, motivational speaker and minister. Mr. White is on a mission to positively influence millions of people through his work, ministry and writing, which currently exceeds 80+ books covering a plethora of

Evangelism 1 on 1

topics including bullying, domestic violence, self-help, history and spirituality.

The Cleveland, Ohio native, a father of five, has overcome many adversities in his life including homelessness and losing his beloved wife to cancer in 1994. Through much heartache and disappointments he discovered a new purpose and passion to use writing as a tool to "plant positive seeds."

Mr. White has developed profound spiritual insight into relationships over the years. Mr. White has written multiple books on the topic of abuse including, In the Ring with Heels On, She's the Boss and Victims of Bullies. Mr. White writes about these and other issues because of the relevance, and prevalence of domestic and other violence. He believes that, "Information plus application equals transformation."

Mr. White is an Evangelist and former pastor. He believes, "God chooses who He uses." He writes, speaks, and ministers to local, national, and international audiences. With an additional 15 new books in the works, Mr. White hopes to give people plenty of "spiritual food" to eat.
White is one of the producers of the documentary "Where's Gina?" about missing children on which he was also narrator.

Timothy White Sr.

He is a co-developer of a tech company (Gsys LLC) that brought blindside technology to vehicles that made billions for the industry, saving countless lives.

He is currently co-hosting a radio show, "Healing the Hurt" on WERE 1490am in Cleveland, Ohio on Thursday evenings 8-10 pm with Host, Rev. Brenda Ware-Abrams.

He is currently on the Advisory Board and is a volunteer instructor at the Juvenile Correction centers in Warrensville Heights and Cleveland, Ohio where his book Seven Signs of Success is being taught.

His book Victims of Bullies is, currently, in the City of Cleveland School system to help stop and make aware of solutions to the issue of bullying.

timwhite55@gmail.com   Timwhitepublishing.com

www.ingramcontent.com/pod-product-compliance
Lightning Source LLC
Chambersburg PA
CBHW032130090426
42743CB00007B/543